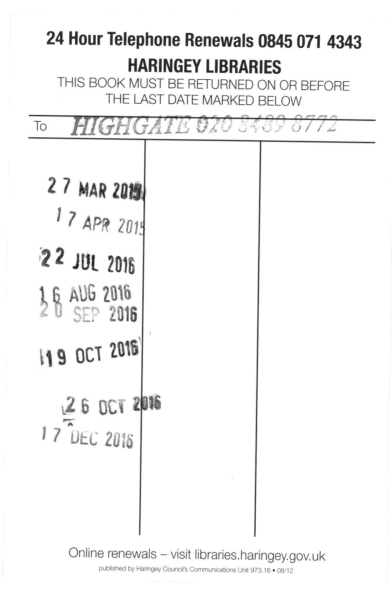

D0258542

LET'S TALK ABOUT
ANIMALS

Illustrated by Britta Teckentrup
Text by Harriet Blackford

Boxer Books®

Contents

What is an animal?

Animals come in all shapes and sizes and colours. Did you know that you are an animal?

Animals eat.

Animals move.

Animals
breathe.

Animals
grow and
have babies.

7

Animals live all over the world

Some animals live in
cold icy places.

Others live in hot
steamy jungles.

Some
live up
in the
air.

And others deep
down in the sea.

Where do
you live?

Animal shapes

There are long, thin snakes.

There are horns and shells with twists and spirals.

There are
fat, round
elephants.

And triangles,
squares
and stars.

What shapes
can you make?

Colours and patterns

Some animals are spotty, some are stripy and some are splotchy.

Some are colourful show-offs.

And others try
not to be seen.
Do you wonder why?

Animals with bones

Bones support you
and give you shape.

Birds have
bones.

Furry or
hairy animals
are called
mammals
and they have
bones.

Reptiles have bones.

Amphibians and fish have bones.

Can you feel your bones?

Animals without bones

Some animals do not have bones. Some have hard crusty skin instead.

Some animals without bones are squishy.

Squishy animals live where it is damp. Some squishy animals grow shells.

How do animals move?

Rabbits run.

Snails slither.

Fish swim.

Dolphins swim
and leap.

Monkeys climb.

Crabs scuttle.

Nothing hurries a sloth!

How do you move?

What do animals eat?

Some eat
only plants.

Some eat other animals.

Some
eat many
different
things.

What do
you like
to eat?

Poo facts

Poo is the waste left over after you have eaten.

A week's worth of elephant poo, called dung, weighs as much as 70 children!

Earthworms leave
curly poos
called casts.

Insects leave a trail
of very tiny poo.

Did you know that cats
almost always
bury their poo?

Animal homes

Wasps make beautiful nests from tiny bits of wood and saliva.

Rabbits dig burrows.

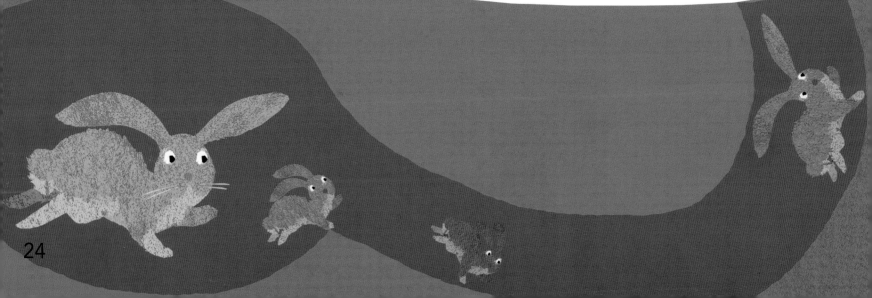

Beavers cut
down trees
to build
themselves
a lodge.

Snails and tortoises carry
their homes with them.

How many of these homes
have you seen?

Animal babies

Some baby animals look like their parents, only smaller.

Some young animals look nothing like their parents.

Have you seen a tadpole change into a frog or a caterpillar change into a butterfly?

Growing up

Some babies have to change a lot before they are grown up.

Some animals have to learn a lot before they are grown up. What have you learned?

Chimpanzee babies copy the grown-ups to find out what to eat.

Tiger cubs learn to hunt by playing with their brothers and sisters.

How animals behave

We use manners so we can get along without fighting.

People shake hands to say hello.

Some people bow.

Angry horses flatten their ears.

Monkeys groom one another to keep friends and make new ones.

Wagging tails mean happy dogs.

Working animals

Guide dogs help blind people move around safely.

Cats on the farm keep rats and mice away from the farmer's grain.

Donkeys and mules pull heavy loads.

This elephant is so strong it can move heavy logs.

Biggest and smallest

The biggest animal in the world is the blue whale. It is as long as 39 people lying down head to toe.

Some tiny creatures in the sea are called zooplankton.

Zooplankton are so small you have to use a microscope to see them. Have you ever used a microscope?

Bizarre and weird

Some animals do some very strange things.

The flying frog stretches out its big webbed feet to glide.

Fireflies can make light in their bodies.

The opossum plays dead if it is frightened.

Archerfish spit at insects and knock them down into the water to eat.

Beware the skunk! It sprays out the worst smell ever.

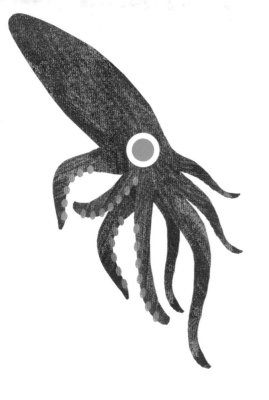

First published in Great Britain in 2009
by Boxer Books Limited.
www.boxerbooks.com

Boxer® is a registered trademark of Boxer Books Limited

This edition published in 2014

The illustrations were prepared using hand-printed paper and digital collage.
The text is set in Avenir.

ISBN 978-1-910126-15-8

1 3 5 7 9 10 8 6 4 2

Printed in China

All of our papers are sourced from managed forests and renewable resources.